THE TONGUES OF A WOMAN

Precious As Gold, Lethal As Lead

"Favour is deceitful, and beauty is vain: but a woman that feareth the LORD, she shall be praised."
(Proverbs 31:20 - KJV).

AB HARRIS

Published by

DAYELight
PUBLISHERS

ISBN: 978-1-953759-45-0

Scripture quotations marked "KJV" are taken from the Holy Bible, King James Version (Public Domain).

I dedicate this book to my wonderful, patient, wise, loving, and amazing wife, Joedale, and our beautiful daughter, Nala; may she one day become the wise and submissive woman who builds and not destroy.

Also, to all the women out there, you are precious, and the Lord made you with great purpose. You have no idea what you are capable of; there is more to you than makeup and eyelashes.

Finally, to all the men who allow folly to consume them, it is time you overcome the tongues of seduction and destruction. Learn the fear of God, and He will keep you.

ACKNOWLEDGMENT

It is my greatest honour to give thanks to God, my Father, and the Lord Jesus Christ. It was through constant prayer and fasting that the wisdom of the Lord was imparted to me to even attempt to write this book.

PREFACE

This book is like no other. The author takes us on a journey of biblical, historical, and personal life experiences to highlight how influential women have been and how they can either built or destroy a man with their tongues; not just a man, but generations. We see how women have caused great men to fall and others to triumph. They have done this through their words and influence that caused life to be either spared or destroyed.

The first five chapters take us on a journey of the tongue of "Asp and Destruction," the tongue of "Seduction," the tongue of "Building," the tongue of "Wisdom," and the tongue of "Submission." The remaining chapters open our eyes to the reality around us and offer deliverance.

Women are a great asset to the world and life itself. Whether good or evil, they have made great contributions to the downfall and sustenance of a people and even kingdoms. It is time they use their tongues to offer life and not death. This book helps and teaches women how to do that. After reading this book, women will know who they want to be and come into the reality of who God created them to be.

CONTENT

INTRODUCTION

The Influence Of Women

A ny man who is afraid to acknowledge the great influence of women is a man who is already deceived. Women have played key roles over the centuries, even from biblical times, in conquering kingdoms, building up men, and preserving lives. Men often underestimate women as being too weak and defenseless. However, women have used these very tools to conquer men.

A foolish man underestimates others without even knowing their capabilities. Are you aware that wars have developed over women? Are you aware that kings have lost their thrones because of women? Are you aware that kingdoms have become one through the marriage of a woman and a man? I believe America has become a society that is ruled by women. Did you think feminism just happened overnight? Do you know that the influence women have over great men have paved the way for them to rise above men? Julia Agusti Filia, the daughter of the Roman Emperor, Augustus Caesar, was known as a clever and viscous woman with a sharp tongue. Her sharp tongue was her tool of influence despite her father denouncing and banishing her.

"How long wilt thou go about, O thou backsliding daughter? for the LORD hath created a new thing in the earth, A woman shall compass a man." (Jeremiah 31: 22 - KJV).

How many people are actually aware of this prophecy in Jeremiah 31:22, that the woman will encompass the man? Unbeknown to many, this scripture is actually telling us that women will take the place of the man. The woman will shelter the man. Is it not from the beginning that the man is the head and the man is the one who would shelter the woman? How is it then that the woman will shelter the man? A shelter is a safe place; somewhere to rest and abide, even as a woman would find a man as her safe place.

However, this prophecy is showing us that a time will come when the woman will take the lead, not that it should be so, but because of the folly of men. Women have caused many men to fall in the past and even presently—*Some to shame and others to their deaths.*

King Solomon, the son of King David, who was beloved of God, was endowed with wisdom and riches to the point that the bible records that there was not a person as wise or as rich as Solomon. His daily preparation of food could probably feed many cities and have leftovers. The man was wealthy and wise, yet God ripped the kingdom out of his hands because of his desire to please his many wives. How ironic, this wise and wealthy king, yet women caused him to lose everything. Was not Solomon wise enough to know that wanting to please his ungodly wives would have cost him everything? But how could it be? What could these women be whispering in the king's ear that would have turned his wisdom to folly? What could they be telling or doing for him that led him to build shrines for their gods? No wonder in Proverbs 31, King Lemuel shared the following words concerning the prophecy his mother taught him:

"Favour is deceitful, and beauty is vain: but a woman that feareth the LORD, she shall be praised." (Proverbs 31:30 - KJV).

Women are neither stupid nor weak as men would think. In fact, God made Eve to be Adam's helpmeet. Would you feel confident with a foolish assistant? Eve was there to support and take care of the garden with Adam. Despite Eve being deceived by the snake (Satan), one must understand that she seemed to be wiser than Adam. Now, if the snake convinced Eve, how was she able to convince Adam? You know he could have said no, but whatever it was that made him agree caused Eve to seem like the wiser person. If you are able to persuade someone, it is either you are smart, or the other person is dumb. Adam was a very wise man; a man who knew the presence of God better than any other man. Therefore at no point am I saying that he was not wise. However, Eve was able to make him take and eat the fruit that he was not supposed to be even looking at. This was his response when asked why he ate the fruit:

"And the man said, The woman whom thou gavest to be with me, she gave me of the tree, and I did eat." (Genesis 3:12 - KJV).

Now the scripture expressly says that the woman saw that the fruit was good. How did she make her husband also see that the fruit was good? What could she have said?

"And when the woman saw that the tree was good for food, and that it was pleasant to the eyes, and a tree to be desired to make one wise, she took of the fruit thereof, and did eat, and gave also unto her husband with her; and he did eat." (Genesis 3: 6 - KJV).

I am sure she was promising her husband, like many woman these days do, that if he does not do this favor, then he is not going to get that special trick on his birthday or anniversary and, even worst, on Valentine's Day. Nonetheless, whatever Eve said convinced Adam.

I am not blaming the woman for the fall of all mankind, but the woman must have said something to the man that made him choose to disobey God and lose his place in the presence of God. What could have convinced Adam, being aware that the day he ate that fruit, he would have died?

"Death and life are in the power of the tongue: and they that love it shall eat the fruit thereof." (Proverbs 18:21 - KJV).

Surely whatever Eve said to Adam caused him to choose death.

Are you still underestimating the woman and her ways? Are you still underestimating the influence of the tongue of the woman? Do you still consider the woman as weak and defenseless?

Do you know that women are very good at turning even the worst situation that life throws at them and getting the best results from it? Over the centuries, women have kept houses, reared children, and are now taking over the society right under our noses. They have turned even children against their own fathers.

I always wonder how a man, even the mightiest man, is disarmed by a beautiful woman. A verse from the song "When a Man Loves a Woman" by Michael Bolton, says,

"…When a man loves a woman, he will turn his back on his best friend." Well, that certainly is the truth; not to mention women causing brothers to become enemies. However, it is not all bad, for we have seen where women have influenced men to do the right things and have saved lives because of their actions. In the same breath, the woman who is able to do and say things to influence a man to lose his kingdom and his life is capable of doing quite the opposite.

The tongue of a woman is a powerful weapon, even more powerful than the golden touch of King Midas. It is not strange at all that marriages have even united kingdoms and people as one force. Athalia, the only woman to rule over Judah without a king, was actually the wife of King Jehoram and daughter of Ahab and Jezebel. Though Israel and Judah were united in wickedness at that time, the marriage united them for a while. Judah and Israel, after the split, never really saw eye to eye as Judah stood more in righteousness than Israel. Nonetheless, her marriage to King Jehoram actually caused Israel and Judah to become one, not physically, but in the same practices that Israel was doing until they killed and/or overthrew her.

Today, Queen Elizabeth has presided over England for decades. She has never given a man the power over her as king since she became Queen at a young age after her father's death. We are somewhat aware of the influence of the daughter over her father. The daddy's girl seems to always get her way, right?

It is very intriguing when you consider: the influence of the wife over the husband, the influence of the daughter over her father, the influence of the sister over the brother, or even the influence of the mother over the son.

Queen Elizabeth and German Chancellor, Angela Dorothea Merkel, are two of the most powerful women in the world. Can you believe that? Has prophecy been fulfilled? However, this did not happen overnight.

In the book of Judges, Deborah was recorded as the only female judge. She was a prophetess of righteousness who judged Israel after they settled into the land. She was one of those women who exuded wisdom. This woman was so wise and filled with understanding that the man, Barack, would not go out to fight Israel's enemies unless she accompanied him. Under her tenure as the only female judge, Israel rested for forty years.

It is a true statement that beside every strong man is a strong woman. The tongue indeed is the strongest muscle in the body because it takes great strength to bend the will of another. While men are lifting heavy weights, the woman has mastered the craft of her tongue.

If there is a man with great potential, trust that a union with the right woman can turn that man into a great individual. How often have we heard the story where a woman takes up a man, who according to society is nothing, and turned him into a king? Very often, if I can recall well. Observe every great man, ministry, and house and tell me if you do not see a woman behind it all. Do not be fooled. Though many women use their tongues in a crafty way, there are those who use their tongues to build men and nations.

The movie "Blindside" depicts the true story of an athlete who became a famous offensive tackle and was adopted into a nuclear family. In this movie, the mother played a more influential role over the young man than the father. She was the one pushing him and making sure he had all he could to fulfill his dreams. I tell you, do not underestimate the tongue of a woman. A wise woman uses her tongue to build, but the foolish uses her tongue to break down and destroy.

In 59 BC, the mother of Augustus Caesar, Atia, lost her husband, but she helped her son to thrive and eventually become the Emperor of Rome. Her tongue had a craft in her son becoming the emperor, though he was not even heir to Julius Caesar, her uncle. She nurtured, raised, and advised her son behind the scenes, and he became the first emperor of Rome.

Not to mention the fact that Helena was mother and advisor to the first Christian emperor, Constantine. These are mothers who have played a significant role in the success of their sons.

How about Plotina, the wife of the emperor Trajan? She was a wealthy and educated noblewoman from what is today the south of France, who used her influence to advance the career of her husband's distant cousin, Hadrian, a young man whom she adored.

The Five Tongues

The character of a woman's heart is worn on the sleeve of her tongue. The image on the cover of the book shows a woman's tongue made of lead, iron, copper, silver, and gold. This represents the five types of tongues a woman possesses that can be used to either build or destroy.

Lead is a very heavy metal that will weigh something down. This depiction speaks to the tongue that will bring destruction. As a man, or anyone overall, you want to run from this type of woman and stay as far from her as possible. She is a danger even to her own self.

As you know, iron is strong, so a woman whose tongue is like iron will build up anything. Whenever you use iron to build, you do so with the hope that it will last. Iron represents strength, durability and sets an

21

expectation of trust. Anyone would trust sitting on an iron chair compared to a plastic or wooden chair.

The part of the tongue that is made of copper is surely going to lead down the path of destruction, for nothing is more poisonous than a seductive tongue. The woman who has mastered the craft of seduction will surely cause great men to fall. This woman will break, divide and conquer; there is no end to her satisfactions.

We now move on to the part of the tongue that is silver, for this is indeed the tongue of a wise woman. A wise woman is surely going to not only build a home, but more so a city and a generation. A woman who knows wisdom is a woman who has learned to cover shame. This is surely the type of woman who births great men and upholds kingdoms.

Finally, the gold tongue is in correlation to the woman with a submissive tongue, for there is nothing purer than fine gold than the Word of God. She covers shame, but most of all, she causes her husband to be a man of adoration. Men will envy other men for this woman, and sons will wish she was their mother; even brothers will envy her and hope she was their sister.

"Behold also the ships, which though they be so great, and are driven of fierce winds, yet are they turned

about with a very small helm, whithersoever the governor listeth." (James 3: 4 - KJV).

As a small rudder is able to steer a great ship, in the same way, the tongues of women have steered great men and have changed the course of history and life itself, whether for good or for evil.

This book will take you on an eye-opening journey about the wisdom, influence, and power of the tongues of the woman.

CHAPTER ONE
"AS LETHAL AS LEAD"

THE TONGUE OF ASP AND DESTRUCTION

"They have sharpened their tongues like a serpent; adders' poison is under their lips. Selah." (Psalm 140:3 - KJV).

The Operations Of This Tongue

The word *asp* is literally speaking about the adder, a common viper or venomous snake. If you know anything about venom, it is a poison that eventually kills you. The end of poison and destruction is death. The woman with this type of tongue will cost you your soul and everything you have ever valued. In fact, a venomous snake only bites to kill, and if you survive, then you should consider yourself blessed.

"For the lips of a strange woman drop as an honeycomb, and her mouth is smoother than oil: But her end is bitter as wormwood, sharp as a two-edged sword." (Proverbs 5:3-4 - KJV).

When we take a deeper look at how the adder functions, we see that this snake lies in wait for its prey, and its main strength is remaining undetected until it is ready to strike. Is it not rather funny how they outplay the role of the damsel in distress in the movies? Now take a look at this damsel in distress, she is always seen as this helpless and stranded woman in need of a hero, but this woman is worst than the seductive tongue. Her art is beyond seduction. She lures you in without having to seduce you and cause you to fall without having to expose all her treasures.

She is like the venomous snake that just wants to get one bite, and then it is over for you. Her fangs are hidden until she is ready to strike. She can come in as the submissive woman, but slowly her fangs will start to show. She can even behave herself in silence, and men will think she is wise, but with subtlety and craftiness, her aim is destruction. Have you noticed how the snake approached the woman in the garden? Have you ever paid attention to its questions?

"And the serpent said unto the woman, Ye shall not surely die: For God doth know that in the day ye eat thereof, then your eyes shall be opened, and ye shall be as gods, knowing good and evil." (Genesis 3:4-5 - KJV).

The snake told the woman something quite the opposite of what God said to her, but it did not just say it directly. It said God knows that the day you eat thereof, then your eyes shall be opened (See Genesis 3:5). It was suggesting that she was not seeing what she thought she was seeing.

If you believe you are not seeing what you know you are seeing, then it is safe to say that you also need to question if you heard what you thought you heard.

There was an incident, and immediately I picked it up. A married man posted a picture on a social media platform, and a woman made the following comment, "Surely the woman that has you is a lucky woman, and your children are blessed to have you as their father." Now many persons would see this as just a harmless compliment, but what happens when she keeps commenting on all his photos or gives him compliments, even when there is no need to? I can recall when I was courting my wife, I had a friend who I did not know in person, but I saw her as a friend. She had indicated her interest once, but we agreed that was not a possibility. One day she made a comment on a photo I posted, and it caught the attention of my now wife.

Her comment was so forward and out there that people would have thought we had something going on. I had to cut and shut down that friendship immediately. She could have destroyed my courtship and caused me to lose my wife even before I had a complete chance.

This woman will hide her true self and make you believe that she is a godly, wise, and submissive woman until she cannot hide her true self anymore. You will not know the true intentions of this woman until it is too late. By that time she would have already achieved her purpose concerning you.

How did the snake approach the woman? The snake approached the woman not as an enemy or something that brought danger and destruction, but rather like a simple concerned person. It pretended to be concerned for poor Adam and Eve, who were told not to eat from the tree, considering they had every other tree to eat from.

Foolish Queen Vashti

In the book of Esther, we read the story of Queen Vashti. She was a queen of Persia and wife to Persian King, Ahasuerus.

"Also Vashti the queen made a feast for the women in the royal house which belonged to king Ahasuerus. On the seventh day, when the heart of the king was merry with wine, he commanded Mehuman, Biztha, Harbona, Bigtha, and Abagtha, Zethar, and Carcas, the seven chamberlains that served in the presence of Ahasuerus the king, To bring Vashti the queen before the king with the crown royal, to shew the people and the princes her beauty: for she was fair to look on. But the queen Vashti refused to come at the king's commandment by his chamberlains: therefore was the king very wroth, and his anger burned in him. Then the king said to the wise men, which knew the times, (for so was the king's manner toward all that knew law and judgment: And the next unto him was Carshena, Shethar, Admatha, Tarshish, Meres, Marsena, and Memucan, the seven princes of Persia and Media, which saw the king's face, and which sat the first in the kingdom;) What shall we do unto the queen Vashti according to law, because she hath not performed the commandment of the king Ahasuerus by the chamberlains? And Memucan answered before the king and the princes, Vashti the queen hath not done wrong to the king only, but also to all the princes, and to all the people that are in all the provinces of the king Ahasuerus. For this deed of the queen shall come abroad unto all women, so that they shall despise their husbands in their eyes, when it shall be reported, the king Ahasuerus commanded Vashti the queen to be brought in before him, but she came not. Likewise shall the ladies of Persia and Media say this day unto all the king's princes, which have heard of the deed of the queen. Thus shall there arise too much contempt and wrath. If it please the king, let there go a royal commandment from him, and let it be written among the laws of the Persians and the Medes, that it be not altered, That Vashti come no more before king Ahasuerus; and let the king give her royal estate unto another that is better than she." (Esther 1:9-19 - KJV).

The above scripture was included to bring about a clearer understanding of this type of woman. The king was having a royal feast where all the noblest of men were invited. He made a request for his wife, the queen, to present herself so he could show off her beauty, but she refused.

This was a foolish woman, and she was bound to bring shame to her husband.

"A virtuous woman *is* a crown to her husband: but she that maketh ashamed *is* as rottenness in his bones." (Proverbs 12:4 - KJV).

This woman was having her own feast for the royal women, and after she refused to come to the king, he was angry and felt disrespected. So the king called his advisors, and they advised him to put the queen away and give her royal estate to another.

At the time of the royal feast, Queen Vashti was also having a feast with the royal women. The wise men concluded that if the other women noticed what Queen Vashti had done, then they would likewise respond to their husbands in the same manner. The men literally said if the king does not use the queen as an example, the other women would think they can be disrespectful to their husbands as well.

One thing is very clear in a kingdom, and that is, no one is higher than the king, not the queen, the princes, or anyone else. When this woman refused to go to the king at his command, she was outright disrespectful. What could cause this woman to think this was right? Her true self was being revealed, and this caused the king to act suddenly to replace her.

One would ask, "Did the king not know this woman was like this?" It is clear that the king did not expect this reaction from her at all. In the book of Esther, we see that it took the women months to prepare Esther as Vashti's replacement. It did not take two, three, or five, but twelve months before Esther could be presented before the king. The custom was that the queen should be a noble woman, but as the scripture says that she who maketh ashamed is as rottenness to a man's bone (See Proverbs 12:4). This woman disrespected the highest authority in the land at that time; he was not only the king, but also her husband. She made him very angry, because this was the last thing he expected from the queen. The king acted wisely because if this woman remained as queen, she would have probably brought down the kingdom before its time.

This woman was queen for a long time, but the king had no idea who she was. When you are summoned by the king, no matter who you are, you should present yourself before the king. Even more so on this day when he wanted all to see how beautiful his wife was, she brought him shame.

This is indeed a foolish woman and, without a doubt, this is one of the main characteristics of this type of woman. The king had this woman as the queen for probably many years, until she caused her folly to bring him shame. The scripture said that the king sent the chamberlain who served in his presence to get the queen, and she refused. She did not do it silently, in his presence only, but before the king's servant.

"Lest thou shouldest ponder the path of life, her ways are moveable, that thou canst not know them." (Proverbs 5:6 - KJV).

Self-Sabotage

Another example of this type of woman would be Saul's daughter. One of King David's wives was Saul's daughter. She despised him because he rejoiced over the Ark of the LORD coming into the city of David.

"And as the ark of the LORD came into the city of David, Michal Saul's daughter looked through a window, and saw king David leaping and dancing before the LORD; and she despised him in her heart." (2 Samuel 6:16 - KJV).

King David was rejoicing because the Ark of the Covenant represented the presence of God. The presence of God was in the city of David, and the king knew that this meant good for him.

"Then David returned to bless his household. And Michal the daughter of Saul came out to meet David, and said, How glorious was the king of Israel to day, who uncovered himself to day in the eyes of the handmaids of his servants, as one of the vain fellows shamelessly uncovereth himself! And David said unto Michal, It was before the LORD, which chose me before thy father, and before all his house, to appoint me ruler over the people of the LORD, over Israel: therefore will I play before the LORD. And I will yet be more vile than thus, and will be base in mine own sight: and of the maidservants which thou hast spoken of, of them shall I be had in honour. Therefore Michal the daughter of Saul had no child unto the day of her death." (2 Samuel 6:20-23 - KJV).

This woman, Michal, considered herself to be wise by telling the king how foolish he looked to uncover himself in the sight of all the people. Her own mouth was her end. Now the king, being a man of God, knew that this woman was going to be trouble for him in the times to come. David knew that she did not regard his rejoicing over the return of the presence of the Lord. As a man who depended on the Lord for everything, he was not going to make this woman hinder him from serving God.

"But he said unto her, Thou speakest as one of the foolish women speaketh. What? shall we receive good at the hand of God, and shall we not receive evil? In all this did not Job sin with his lips." (Job 2:10 - KJV).

The above scripture states what Job said to his wife after she told him to curse God and die because of the suffering that came upon him. Job rebuked her as a foolish woman, for she wanted him to sin against God. In the same manner, the serpent used crafty words that convinced Eve to sin against God.

Any woman who uses her tongue or any other means to convince you to sin against God is surely signing you over to death and destruction.

So far we see that for some reason, these women have found themselves in some noble positions. However, they are there as a result of their crafty tongues, just like the snake. How do you think the snake gets its prey? It achieves this through patience and subtlety.

Wicked Queen Jezebel

In the book of Kings, we learn about King Ahab and Queen Jezebel. This is the Jezebel that many women wish not to be likened to, but who can blame them. However, a number of women are overtaken by this character.

Jezebel was the Queen of Israel in the time of the prophet Elijah. She introduced the worship of Baal and literally killed some prophets of the true God, to the point where

36

Obadiah, the servant of King Ahab, had to hide some of the prophets in caves and feed them. She prostituted the land of Israel to false gods and attracted the judgment of the true God upon Israel.

Though her husband Ahab was the king, Jezebel was calling the shots. There was an incident where King Ahab wanted the vineyard of Naboth, but he refused to give it up because it was his inheritance. This is how Jezebel handled the situation.

"And Ahab came into his house heavy and displeased because of the word which Naboth the Jezreelite had spoken to him: for he had said, I will not give thee the inheritance of my fathers. And he laid him down upon his bed, and turned away his face, and would eat no bread. But Jezebel his wife came to him, and said unto him, Why is thy spirit so sad, that thou eatest no bread? And he said unto her, Because I spake unto Naboth the Jezreelite, and said unto him, Give me thy vineyard for money; or else, if it please thee, I will give thee another vineyard for it: and he answered, I will not give thee my vineyard. And Jezebel his wife said unto him, Dost thou now govern the kingdom of Israel? Arise, and eat bread, and let thine heart be merry: I will give thee the vineyard of Naboth the Jezreelite. So she wrote letters in Ahab's name, and sealed them with his seal, and sent the letters unto the elders and to the nobles that were in his city, dwelling with Naboth. And she wrote in the

letters, saying, Proclaim a fast, and set Naboth on high among the people: And set two men, sons of Belial, before him, to bear witness against him, saying, Thou didst blaspheme God and the king. And then carry him out, and stone him, that he may die." (1 Kings 21:4-10 - KJV).

Jezebel called false witnesses to testify against Naboth and caused him to be killed. This type of woman causes death and destruction. Can you imagine if Queen Vashti had gotten her way or Michal, Saul's daughter? You may be thinking, but is she not a good wife who is just giving her husband his heart's desires? Why do you think she was in charge of Israel and not the king?

"Now therefore send and gather all Israel to me at Mount Carmel, and the 450 prophets of Baal and the 400 prophets of Asherah, who eat at Jezebel's table." (1 Kings 18:19 - KJV).

Notice how the scripture said the prophets of Baal who eat at Jezebel's table? This woman had caused false gods and false prophets to come into the kingdom and exalted them over God and the things of God. The prophet Elijah was the one who said this statement before he challenged the prophets of Baal on Mount Carmel.

Indeed her mouth is as Asp and filled with poison. After Elijah had witnessed the power of God and fire coming down from heaven, this woman Jezebel threatened him to the point where he desired to die. Her words pierced him even though it was sent through a messenger.

"Ahab told Jezebel all that Elijah had done, and how he had killed all the prophets with the sword. Then Jezebel sent a messenger to Elijah, saying, So may the gods do to me and more also, if I do not make your life as the life of one of them by this time tomorrow. Then he was afraid, and he arose and ran for his life and came to Beersheba, which belongs to Judah, and left his servant there." (1 Kings 19:1-3 - KJV).

Elijah became afraid of this woman for she had killed many other prophets, yet he was not afraid of the king. The threat of her words pierced the prophet to his soul, and fear overtook him.

Surely this is a tongue of destruction. Now these women were obviously beautiful, for they were all queens. However, they all demonstrated the tongue of Asp and destruction. These types of women are like snakes who hide until it is time to attack their preys. There will come a point where you will realize that they are biting you; their words towards you become destructive; and their desire is to rule over you, but this is accomplished through craftiness. At first they make themselves appear very useful until they have gotten themselves in the right position and place.

They are the masters of manipulation and control. If they cannot have control, then your life is going to be miserable. This is true not only for men, but also for their friends and family. They will use their words to destroy you, and whenever you start catching up to them, they turn your own friends and family against you.

Personal Experience

There was an incident that happened to me some years ago, just when I was seeking to get closer to the Lord. I had just received the baptism of the Holy Spirit and wanted to learn more about God. So, somehow I became friends with this lady who I believed was very gifted. I thought she was a woman of God and that God was using her to operate in the gifts of the Spirit. So, I started going to her church with her; a prophetic church that did a lot of deliverance.

I ended up inviting my friend to this church, and we became a group that was hungry for God. But there was just something wrong about this woman. She had a bitter and unforgiving spirit and a mouth that needed deliverance. She would speak badly about the pastor of the church, and we knew that something was wrong. To make matters worse, she fragmented the scriptures and gave false revelations which I called "Revelytions." She told so many lies about her experiences; we wanted to have those experiences, but they were all lies. There came a point when I heard a voice telling me she was a witch,

40

but I had never experienced this before or thought witches were in the church. She would try to challenge my wisdom and say she does not care if I have the gift of wisdom, God made her head over me. Well, God did not give me that memo, so I started paying attention.

One day, something happened and I got a phone call from my friends. They wanted to meet me and I told them I knew why they were calling. When I told them why, they were shocked that we all were getting this silently in our spirits from God.

I distanced myself as by this time I was being warned in dreams about her. She tried to set my friends against me, not knowing that we already knew the truth.

This woman wanted to rule over us, and half of what was said and done is not mentioned, but this is the example of this type of tongue and its powers of death and destruction.

Encouragement

If you are reading this book and you are a woman with some of these characteristics, you need to be delivered by the Blood of Jesus Christ. If you have a friend and you see this type of character in him/her, you really need to open your eyes; and if you are a man who is with this type of woman, you need to run.

Another aspect of this woman is that she is a gossiper and full-on contentious.

"It is better to dwell in the corner of the housetop, than with a brawling woman and in a wide house." (Proverbs 25:24 - KJV).

A contentious woman takes away peace, and once you have no peace, it is like living in hell. There is no break from the constant torment and nagging.

The thing to be mindful of is that with this woman, she will meet all your desires, and you will be so swept off your feet. As a man, you will not notice her true self until it is too late. Her true self is a nagging, gossiping, home-wrecking, manipulating, controlling, and destructive woman and, just like the snake, she is lurking and waiting to get just one bite.

Surely this type of woman will bring you to an end physically and spiritually. A woman who causes you to become a reproach before God is surely of this tongue. Deliverance comes through the Lord Jesus Christ and knowing His Word as it is the only way to be freed from this tongue.

CHAPTER TWO
"AS POISONOUS AS COPPER"

THE TONGUE OF SEDUCTION

"For she hath cast down many wounded: yea, many strong men have been slain by her." (Proverbs 7:26 - KJV).

The Operations Of This Tongue

Do you know those plants that are arrayed beautifully and then suddenly as an insect comes by it is caught by the plant? This depicts a type of woman who uses her tongue and ways to lure men. Unlike the tongue of Asp that lurks and waits, this woman lures her prey with seduction and beauty, but she is very vain.

She relies on her charm and beauty a lot, and is as destructive as the tongue of Asp and destruction. She does not normally use her tongue to rule over men, but she uses it to get them to do what she desires. It is like controlling the heart of the man rather than his kingdom and having access to his possessions rather than full control over everything. Still, his end is death and destruction. This woman is a tool to many evil men and also a great danger to great men.

I once met a woman on a bus, and we ended up exchanging contacts because she professed to be a backslider who needed help; that was a BIG mistake. At that time, I was much more bold and eager about ministering to people, so my intentions were very pure. She shared that she was in the church and struggling to get to the place she wanted to be. I was very excited about reaching and encouraging people in the Lord, so we became friends. I had to go away for a season, and we maintained contact. I made it clear that I was not interested in a relationship, and at that time, I was just telling her about the Lord and trying to pray with and help her through. After some time, she began pressing me daily about seeing me so we can talk about God and she could have a friend to strengthen her. Let me tell you this from now, if you are a Christian male, do not invite a female over at any time to study the Bible; the same goes for the females.

This young lady was pressing me, and I kept shutting her down, until she called me one day and sounded a bit low, so I told her she could come over. She got to my home very fast. While there, we were just hanging out, but in my mind I was praying for strength, among other things. Then suddenly we were getting closer, and I thought she wanted to kiss me, so I tried to kiss her; that was quite foolish on my part. When she turned away, I felt relieved like she was not here for that, until about fifteen minutes later, she made her move on me. That was such a seductive move that I was totally caught off guard. We ended up kissing, and then things started moving so fast. She started saying some seductive things, and I do not know where the strength came from, but I pushed her away and told her I could not sin against God. After that, I called a cab for her and told her to have a nice life.

While going out the door, she wanted me to hug her, and I just said goodbye. I felt so bad that I almost had sex with her and sin against God. What took place that day should not even have happened. This is the case with the tongue of seduction; it plays on you until you are caught in its web, just as a spider that weaves its web with the hope that its prey will be caught in it.

The only thing worse than a wicked man is a wicked woman. You see, men can be very wicked and very brutal, but a woman, when she masters a thing, no man can contest her. As I said, this type of woman presses a man through her seductive ways and tongue. These women are often the most envious and self-seeking amongst all other women.

It is very common for you to see a seductive woman going after married men. The one who goes after single men is either married or sees something that she wants from a particular man.

A woman who pursues a married man has no morals, neither does she respect herself or the other woman. A married woman who pursues another man is lower than a harlot. This may sound like a very harsh statement, but many are quick to cast aside the woman who is openly a harlot, but not those who are secretly so. It is hard to believe that a married woman of all women would play the role of a harlot secretly.

Let us take a look at young Joseph from the scriptures in the book of Genesis. He was sold into Egypt by his jealous brothers, but God was with Joseph. So while he was in Egypt, he prospered instead of dying.

"And it came to pass from the time that he had made him overseer in his house, and over all that he had, that the LORD blessed the Egyptian's house for Joseph's sake; and the blessing of the LORD was upon all that he had in the house, and in the field. And he left all that he had in Joseph's hand; and he knew not ought he had, save the bread which he did eat. And Joseph was a goodly person, and well favoured." (Genesis 39:5-6 - KJV).

Joseph was favored in the eyes of Potiphar, an officer of Pharaoh and captain of the guard. Now, because Joseph was favored of the Lord, he was a prosperous man in Egypt to the point where Potiphar made him master over his household. Potiphar made him head over everything in his house, and he could have anything he desired, but not his master's wife.

Potiphar's Adulterous Wife

Now the scripture gives us a detailed scenario of how Potiphar's wife, a married woman, tried to cast herself at this young man with her seductive and deceptive ways.

"And it came to pass after these things, that his master's wife cast her eyes upon Joseph; and she said, Lie with me. But he refused, and said unto his master's wife, Behold, my master wotteth not what is with me in the house, and he hath committed all that he hath to my hand; There is none greater in this house than I; neither hath he kept back anything from me but thee, because thou art his wife: how then can I do this great wickedness, and sin against God? And it came to pass, as she spake to Joseph day by day, that he hearkened not unto her, to lie by her, or to be with her. And it came to pass about this time, that Joseph went into the house to do his business; and there was none of the men of the house there within. And she caught him by his garment, saying, Lie with me: and he left his garment in her hand, and fled, and got him out. And it came to pass, when she saw that he had left his garment in her hand, and was fled forth, That she called unto the men of her house, and spake unto them, saying, See, he hath brought in an Hebrew unto us to mock us; he came in unto me to lie with me, and I cried with a loud voice:

49

And it came to pass, when he heard that I lifted up my voice and cried, that he left his garment with me, and fled, and got him out. And she laid up his garment by her, until his lord came home." (Genesis 39:7-16 - KJV).

The seductive woman is very persistent; she does not give up if the man resists her. The scripture says the woman came to Joseph and demanded that he should lie with her. She did not want him to only lie with her, but if you take a closer look at verse 10, it says that he would not listen to her to lie with her nor to be with her.

She did not just want Joseph to lie with her, but to also be with her. Joseph, however, was a wise man, as we can see. He told her plainly that she wanted him to do this wickedness against his master and, most importantly, his God. He asked how he could do such a wicked thing, but the woman tried after him day by day. It is sad to say that a lot of men would have probably been seduced by her, but not the man who fears the Lord God.

A seductive woman hates being rejected. We see in the scripture where this woman got to the point that she grabbed Joseph, who fled from her and left his coat in her hands. It is better to flee from a seductive woman than to be caught in her webs.

"And I find more bitter than death the woman, whose heart is snares and nets, and her hands as bands: whoso

pleaseth God shall escape from her; but the sinner shall be taken by her." (Ecclesiastes 7:26 - KJV).

Here is a very interesting point that I want to make. When a seductive woman cannot get you to fall into her traps, she will start to hate you, and any opportunity she gets, she will destroy you. Look at this married woman, whose husband is a respectable man in Egypt; she literally went after a mere slave boy, but those who are spiritual will know that things are deeper than what we know it to be. However, since she was not able to get him to sleep with her, she told a lie that caused him to be thrown into prison.

Joseph was a very wise man to not sleep with Potiphar's wife, although he could have reported it to his master from day one, but that was probably another wise decision. This seductive woman would have found a way to spin it on Joseph, for her own husband was already in her webs. As we can clearly see, this is an adulterous woman.

A number of men have fallen as prey to these women, and it is because they are very foolish; they are not victims but rather fools.

I find it rather interesting that whenever a man in the United States especially is running for some political position, there is always a woman who can say they were molested by these men. I am not downplaying that there are some very dirty and disgusting men out there who are doing these things, but is it just a coincidence that these men always find themselves in these accusations? To make it worst, most of these men are married.

"The way of an eagle in the air; the way of a serpent upon a rock; the way of a ship in the midst of the sea; and the way of a man with a maid. Such is the way of an adulterous woman; she eateth, and wipeth her mouth, and saith, I have done no wickedness." (Proverbs 30:19-20 - KJV).

When a seductive woman is done with you, she wipes her mouth and says, "I have done nothing." Do you think a spider feels bad for the foolish prey that is caught in its webs? Then why should a seductive woman feel bad for the prey that are caught by her seduction?

When the devil wants to bring down a mighty man, his greatest tool is the seductive woman.

Seductive Delilah

In the book of Judges, we learn of the well-known Samson, a man of great supernatural strength which he possessed by the Spirit of God. This man was feared by all his enemies because he was supernaturally strong and would always defeat them. No matter what army of people was sent to Samson, he would destroy them all.

This mighty man, who was anointed by God, was brought low because of a seductive woman. Samson was given one command, and that was to not defile himself with wine, nor come to the dead carcass, nor put a razor to his head **(See Judges 16)**.

It is very interesting that Samson had a thing for the Philistine women. I am not sure whether they were more beautiful than the Israeli women, but as one of my friends once said, "God does not waste our mistakes." So God used Samson's weakness to still deliver Israel at his death.

Now let us examine the scripture taken from Judges 16 closely.

"And it came to pass afterward, that he loved a woman in the valley of Sorek, whose name was Delilah. And the lords of the Philistines came up unto her, and said unto her, Entice him, and see wherein his great strength lieth, and by what means we may prevail against him, that we may bind him to afflict him; and we will give thee every one of us eleven hundred pieces of silver. And Delilah said to Samson, Tell me, I pray thee, wherein thy great strength lieth, and wherewith thou mightest be bound to afflict thee." (Judges 16:4-6 - KJV).

Here we see that Samson loved this woman, who his enemies were setting up to betray him. Why were they doing this? Well, for a lot of silver, if you should think about it, but Samson's enemies desired to prevail over him, and the only way to get that done was by a woman to seduce him.

Delilah wasted no time. In verse 6, the woman just came out asking him directly where his great strength lay. She did not just ask him where his strength lay, but she also asked how they could bind him to do him harm. Samson was either very seduced or he had no wisdom at all. Either way, this woman never gave up until she destroyed him.

Now I want to show you the persistence of the seductive woman. After Samson lied about the source of his strength three times, this was what the woman said to him.

"And she said unto him, How canst thou say, I love thee, when thine heart is not with me? thou hast mocked me these three times, and hast not told me wherein thy great strength lieth. And it came to pass, when she pressed him daily with her words, and urged him, so that his soul was vexed unto death; That he told her all his heart, and said unto her, There hath not come a razor upon mine head; for I have been a Nazarite unto God from my mother's womb: if I be shaven, then my

54

strength will go from me, and I shall become weak, and be like any other man. And when Delilah saw that he had told her all his heart, she sent and called for the lords of the Philistines, saying, Come up this once, for he hath shewed me all his heart. Then the lords of the Philistines came up unto her, and brought money in their hand." (Judges 16:15-18 - KJV).

The name Delilah literally means lovelorn or seductive. Did this woman really ask Samson how he can say he loved her when he mocked her three times? Did Samson not see the signs? No one can escape a seductive woman, except he who pleases God.

Delilah pressed Samson daily until he became vexed within, and he poured out his heart before her, and without hesitation, she immediately went to collect her reward. She was the one who cut the locks off his head while he lay on her lap. The seductive woman, as I said above, is a tool in the devil's hands to destroy strong men.

I have been emphasizing that the seductive woman is very persistent. She presses you in every way that a man can be pressed and tempted. When she finally gets her way, she will destroy you.

While the woman who has the tongue of Asp and destruction will destroy you for she wants to take your place, the seductive woman will eat you up just like the black widow eats her mate. This woman is by far the worst among them all; she will cause you to sin against God the most. She is not interested in ruling over you or taking your position. She is just interested in breaking you down just as enzymes break down food.

I was once bitten by a woman like this. I take full responsibility for my actions, and I am not blaming this woman for what happened, for I knew the spirits that were at work. Being warned of this, I should not have given in to youthful folly.

Personal Experience

A year before this happened, I received a prophetic word that it was not fornication that caused Satan to fall but rather pride. Just days before I got bitten by this woman, I was warned by a prophet that he saw me fall. Instead of going down in prayer and begging God for mercy, I told him I would not let that happen to me. What a fool I was to not see pride going before me.

One day after coming off work, I went to check on a sister of mine. At the time she was just a sister based on the importance of our friendship, but glory to God, she is also now a sister in the Lord.

When I arrived at her room, she had a friend there who I had never seen before. The moment I saw this young lady, she caught my attention. It was crazy, but I know most people can relate to this. This young lady looked like the woman I had desired when I was in my teen years. She was what one would call their dream girl. I tried my best not to engage her, but we introduced ourselves, and I was there for a moment, and then she left and I honestly never expected to see her again. What a coincidence that I would actually come upon this girl at a point where I was seeking God so much and expecting a great encounter from Him.

Just like the first time, I went to look for my sister and again she was there. We were all there talking; something came up in the conversation, and my sister pointed out that I was a man of God and they then moved on from there.

It so happened that sometime after that, this young lady was in some serious trouble and I was there. She said to me, "Aren't you a man of God? Can you pray for us about this?" I prayed for them, and things turned out exactly how I asked the Lord to intervene.

Have you ever felt good for doing good but stupid at the same time because you know that a strange fire has come knocking at your door?

Now at this point, this girl ended up working at the same place I was working and lived in the same apartment I was living. If this did not spell danger, then I do not know what danger was.

I ended up training this young lady on this job, and we were getting close without me even noticing. I would always look up and see her looking at me; she would always try to play with me through subliminal words.

How could I not have seen this creeping up on me? How could I be so blind? This young lady was really close to me. A group of us would go out together, and she was always there. Trouble was right up my alley, and I was too blind by my own pride to see it.

When I felt like she was getting close and I needed to do something about it, I went on a fast to break off all the feelings I was developing as she was not saved, and I would only pursue a woman I was seeking to marry. After I completed this short fast, I went to her, sat her down, and we talked. I told her we had to stop; we could not let this go any further, and she was literally crying. I felt so bad, but I made up my mind that I had to make this stop. I honestly wished it had really stopped then and I had stood by my words.

Later on that day, I fell asleep, and I was frightened out of my sleep and wondering if she was going to try and harm herself. Why would I think that? I went to her door and knocked to check on her, and she was still crying. So out of feeling guilty, I invited her to come to my apartment to watch television as I was still sleepy.

We went back there, and I was trying to sleep, but she had one of those talking spells. During this time, about three people came to check on me. One of those persons was my best friend, who told me that he felt like I was about to do something stupid, and I told him that I was really trying to sleep, and I was being honest.

I had no desire to have sex or sin against God; my mind was not on sex at all. I was that young man who really had a heart to please God. I really wanted to do God's will with all my heart.

While this young lady was talking to me, she said something to me that day, that up to this point I cannot tell you what she said, or maybe it was how she said it. When she said that, something in me just changed. It was like my mind got clouded, and my flesh became hungry. I was living pure and consecrated for so many years up until this point. Whatever she said ended in us having sex that night. The moment I ejaculated, I felt a rip in my left side. That was way more spiritual than it was physical. It was like virtue and strength left my body.

After that incident, the Lord kept speaking to me in some ways that really shook me. The same prophet said that he hoped the next time he saw me, I would be the same strong man he met. Then one of the men I was working with said to me that since I started hanging around women, I did not look as strong as I once did. Now this man was not a Christian, nor did he understand that God was talking through him.

God was talking to me; He was trying to rescue me from the webs of seduction. My heart was broken. At the same time, something was happening around me, and I knew that it was because of what had befallen me. A sister in the faith also was going through something terrible, and I want to pause for a moment to say this to the person reading this book: God does not waste your mistakes. My best friend, who knew me before this experience, saw how God was lifting me through this, and the Lord saved him. My sister, who I mentioned earlier, also got saved a year or so after. The young lady who the Lord used me to help strengthen while she was down is now a stronger Christian the last time I saw her. God will not waste your mistakes.

Now back to the story. I was in this young lady's web, but I did not blame her. I knew this was the devil trying to destroy me. What opened my eyes was a dream this young lady had. I am the type of person who takes dreams and visions very seriously.

During this time, I was trying to strengthen myself in the Lord and had encouraged her to do the same. She then

60

said to me that she was trying, but she felt like something was trying to hold on to her mind, to not let her believe or accept God's Word. She then had a dream of the Jezebel spirit holding her head, and she asked Jezebel if she was the one destroying the people of God's marriages, and Jezebel said yes.

Now these were two spiritual things that were revealed to me, and I knew that I had to pray and seek the Lord for an escape. Finally, she said to me that she felt like she was Delilah and that she was causing me to sin against God. That hit me so hard.

Bam! I knew that I was being attacked by the enemy. The women who are manifesting this behavior and characteristics are being influenced by these spirits that are the origin of these characters. Interestingly, I was sharing with a woman of God while I was in the situation, and she said exactly the same thing that I just concluded. Glory to God, I am over this battle and severed from that tongue of seduction. The enemy almost destroyed me completely, but during that time, the Lord was delivering me.

All this was truly a moment where I learned and understood so much more and am now able to be sharing this with you.

"The mouth of strange women is a deep pit: he that is abhorred of the LORD shall fall therein." (Proverbs 22:14 - KJV).

Devious Herodias

Finally, let us look at the example of John the Baptist, the prophet who was sent before the Lord Jesus Christ to prepare the way before His first coming.

Now take this prophet, a preacher of righteousness, who told King Herod that it was not lawful for him to have the wife of his brother, Phillip. Herod was afraid to harm John, for he knew he was a true prophet, but the woman cared not, for John was causing problems for her.

"For Herod himself had sent forth and laid hold upon John, and bound him in prison for Herodias' sake, his brother Philip's wife: for he had married her. For John had said unto Herod, It is not lawful for thee to have thy brother's wife. Therefore Herodias had a quarrel against him, and would have killed him; but she could not: For Herod feared John, knowing that he was a just man and an holy, and observed him; and when he heard him, he did many things, and heard him gladly. And when a convenient day was come, that Herod on his birthday made a supper to his lords, high captains, and chief estates of Galilee; And when the daughter of the said Herodias came in, and danced, and pleased Herod and them that sat with him, the king said unto

62

the damsel, Ask of me whatsoever thou wilt, and I will give it thee. And he sware unto her, Whatsoever thou shalt ask of me, I will give it thee, unto the half of my kingdom." (Mark 6: 17-23 - KJV).

The scripture said the woman would have killed John, but the king feared, knowing he was just and holy. The tongue of seduction is always waiting patiently for its victims to fall in its trap.

Herodias' daughter danced for Herod on his birthday in front of all his officials, and she pleased the king to the point that he promised her that she could get whatever she asked, even the half of his kingdom.

Seduction is truly wicked. How is this even possible that a lap dance could have gotten the king to a place where he was ready to give away half of his kingdom? Foolish men underestimate the influence of a woman.

The kings swore that he would do this, and he did so before all his captains and chief people. In the verses following verse 23, the young lady went to her mother, and her mother told her to ask for the head of John the Baptist. She could have had half the kingdom, but no; she wanted to get rid of the man who found out her seductive ways.

So we have truly seen that a woman with the tongue of seduction is very dangerous, and if a man is not covered and protected by the Lord, he is in danger. Only the man who pleases the Lord can escape this woman.

Encouragement

If you are reading this book and you are a woman who believes you have been under this spirit that causes the tongue of seduction, you need to ask the Lord for deliverance. Also, if you are a man who is under the control of a seductive woman, then you need to run for your life to the Lord Jesus Christ.

"As a jewel of gold in a swine's snout, so is a fair woman which is without discretion." (Proverbs 11:22 - KJV).

We cannot be too willing to accept toxic and deadly behaviors as our true selves. After reading this chapter, you should really look over your life for revelations you have received and then act upon them.

CHAPTER THREE
"AS STRONG AS IRON"

THE TONGUE OF BUILDING

The Operations Of This Tongue

The popular phrase, "Behind every great man there's a great woman" that was adopted by the feminist movement in the 1960's/70's is almost correct. In fact, they should have said "beside" every great man is a great woman, for God never placed Eve behind Adam, though he was her head. She was taken from his side, not his toes.

Does a married man not hold the hands of his wife when they are together, or is the woman behind the man? Does a man who protects his woman put her behind or closer to him? When a man and woman are getting married, have you ever seen the woman standing behind the man at the altar?

A strong woman does not mind being in her husband's shadow because it does not take away her strength; she knows that she is always by his side in strength, and she is not in his shadow. She is one with him, though she esteems him with respect and endows him with uplifting words that cause him to believe that he can accomplish anything with her as his wife.

The strength of a woman should never be measured by her profession but rather her abilities and character. People often assume that because women drive trucks and join the army, they are strong. This is a worldly misconception of strength. One should never assume that because a woman is strong, she is not going to be submissive. Some women only know how to be strong by the world's idea of strength, but a strong woman knows how to submit to her husband in respect and honor.

The major difference between the tongue of building and the tongue of wisdom is that wisdom knows how to preserve and protect what was built, and the building knows how to make something despite the obstacles and can endure.

A strong tongue that is not tamed can cause destruction. In the same way it takes strength to build, strength can also destroy.

When a kingdom is going to be built, a strong woman is there to help build it. When an empire is going to be great, a strong woman is there to ensure that it is a great empire.

These are the women we do not see or hear sometimes, but they are always there encouraging their husbands who turn out to be great men and build great empires.

These are the wives of many men of God that you see with great ministries. Men who become presidents, premiers, and sometimes great businessmen have these women as wives since day one.

A man of God, who was like a father to me, shared a story of his wife, who was also like a mother to me. His wife had quit her job to stay home and take care of the kids and manage the house while he pursued his ministry. That was the ministry under which I came to accept the Lord. Her children are now professionals in their different fields, and they are still strong in their faith, serving the Lord. This woman of God was at the top of her profession when she decided to give it all up to stay home with her children and stand by her husband's side in ministry. The ministry is over thirty years now, and I have seen the greatness of it.

This is a strong and wise woman. I have been blessed by her words that helped to build me up. When I was in my teenage years, she contributed greatly to the development of my confidence and character.

"Who can find a virtuous woman? For her price is far above rubies. The heart of her husband doth safely trust in her, so that he shall have no need of spoil. She will do him good and not evil all the days of her life. She seeketh wool, and flax, and worketh willingly with

her hands. She is like the merchants' ships; she bringeth her food from afar." (Proverbs 31:10-14 - KJV).

Indeed she is a virtuous woman and more precious than rubies. Any man who desires to be great must carefully choose his wife; for the tongue of the woman can either build or destroy. The scripture says she will do good and not evil all the days of her life. I have watched this woman of God, and she always builds up her husband; even when he is not present, she will not tear him down.

Something I have noticed is that women like this have a motherly character, and they tend to show great nurturing skills. Men, these women are not your mothers; a woman who is like a great mother can be likened to the eagle that carries her young on her wings and teaches them to fly.

Another example is this woman of God, who I affectionately call Lady Wisdom. This woman of God once did something I thought was so profound that now I can surely say she possesses the tongue of building. There was a point in my life when I just received the baptism of the Holy Spirit, and the Lord was showing me a number of spiritual things. During this time, I was having some trouble with my leaders. I felt they were coming against me, but she took me aside and read me a scripture from Psalm 119. Honestly, what she did lifted me up to the point where I was able to grow without further conflict.

Furthermore, she took me to be a part of the ministry she was heading, and during that time, the gift in me was being nurtured into something great that is with me to this very day.

She is also a wise woman because I later came to the knowledge that that was the reason a number of young people were encouraged to continue in the church and use their gifts to glorify the Lord.

At the battle of Dyrrachium in 1081, it was the strength of Princess Sichelgata of Salerno, the wife of Robert Guiscard, who was the leader of the Norman Army, that stopped the Norman soldiers from fleeing. This woman confronted her fellow soldiers and urged them to stop fleeing. When they would not listen and continued running, she grasped a long spear and charged at full gallop against them. This brought them to their senses, and they went back to fight. Because of her boldness and strength, she was able to encourage the entire army to victory. A woman who is able to move the heart of an army of mostly men is not a normal woman.

The point here is that this woman was able to encourage an entire army to stand and fight, and they got the victory. There are instances where queens were left in charge of the kingdoms while the kings went to war. These women had to take charge of the kingdoms and keep them running while their husbands sought victory.

Do you think that was easy for them? Do you think it was easy to keep people in line, some of whom had intentions to take over the kingdom if the king should die? No, it was not easy at all, but they got it done. Some of these kings who came from victory came and saw their kingdoms in good shape, and for those who died, those women never gave up the fight until death.

These women are visionaries and are able to bring even far-reaching dreams out of men, things that seem impossible to the men they are building up, and they will not seek to take the credit.

Among this category of women are those who are barren. A number of barren women out there are able to help build their husband's dreams but are not able to give them children (I will provide further insights on this in chapter six). However, these women bring forth great men. How do I know this? It was the barron Sarah who brought forth Isaac; the barren Rebecca who brought forth Jacob and Esau; the barren Rachael who brought forth Joseph; the barren Manoah's wife who brought forth Samson; the barren Hannah who brought forth Samuel and the barren Elizabeth who brought forth John the Baptist.

Deborah, A Mother And Judge

Now let us take a look at the prophetess Deborah, who was described as a mother in Israel. This woman of God sat under a palm tree, between Ramah and Bethel in mount Ephraim, judging the children of Israel. She was the only female judge recorded in the Bible, and she was highly respected. She was also the wife of Lapidoth, who the Bible did not really provide any further information about; this woman never ruled over her husband, nor did she make him feel any less by her role in Israel.

Her strength was one to admire. Barak, as the man who God called to deliver Israel out of the hands of the Canaanites, would not go to battle without her.

"And Barak said unto her, If thou wilt go with me, then I will go: but if thou wilt not go with me, then I will not go. And she said, I will surely go with thee: notwithstanding the journey that thou takest shall not be for thine honour; for the LORD shall sell Sisera into the hand of a woman. And Deborah arose, and went with Barak to Kedesh." (Judges 4:8-9 - KJV).

The Lord used this woman to judge Israel for forty years. During the times of judges was when Israel moved into the land that the Lord had promised them. Joshua had died by this time. The entire nation was still in the building phase, and the Lord had to use this woman, one among many men, to judge Israel. She was one of the second long-serving judges.

"A wife of noble character is her husband's crown, but a disgraceful wife is like decay in his bones." (Proverbs 12:4 - NIV).

Jael The Woman Of Honor

Another woman who is found in the same chapter of Judges is Jael. Jael was the wife of Heber, who destroyed Sisera, the captain of Jabin's army. Jabin was the king of Canaan.

"And Jael went out to meet Sisera, and said unto him, Turn in, my lord, turn in to me; fear not. And when he had turned in unto her into the tent, she covered him with a mantle. And he said unto her, Give me, I pray thee, a little water to drink; for I am thirsty. And she opened a bottle of milk, and gave him drink, and covered him. Again he said unto her, Stand in the door of the tent, and it shall be, when any man doth come and enquire of thee, and say, Is there any man here? that thou shalt say, No. Then Jael Heber's wife took a nail of the tent, and took an hammer in her hand, and went softly unto him, and smote the nail into his temples, and fastened it into the ground: for he was fast asleep and weary. So he died. And, behold, as Barak pursued Sisera, Jael came out to meet him, and said unto him, Come, and I will shew thee the man whom

thou seekest. And when he came into her tent, behold, Sisera lay dead, and the nail was in his temples. (Judges 4:18-22 - KJV).

Now this woman never had it in her intention to take the glory for this victory, neither was she his wife, but she did her part in defeating the enemies of Israel. She did not seek to take the glory for it but rather showed Barak that she had killed Sisera.

A strong woman seeks to build up, but a foolish woman seeks to destroy and tear down. Women have to choose who they would rather be, and men who seek to be great must take these things into serious consideration. The foolish woman will even destroy her own legacy.

"She maketh fine linen, and selleth *it*; and delivereth girdles unto the merchant." (Proverbs 31:24 - KJV).

From this scripture you can see the women who makes great and creative businesses out of nothing. I saw a video once of a lady in Africa who started a business from literally nothing. She made products out of recycled garbage.

Undeniably we have seen these women starting businesses after overcoming teenage pregnancy and even after having five or more children. They are builders; it is in their nature to build up.

My wife, for example, is one of these women. God has given her great wisdom, and if I could invest every cent I made in my wife, I know that we would have a multi-million dollar corporation. She is the planner, she has so many ideas, and I have even seen her help those around her build themselves.

Personal Experience

Before I decided to marry my wife, I went to seek the Lord to ensure that she was the right one. I saw her wisdom and the fear of God in her life, but I still wanted to be sure because, as a man of God once said, "Even the one can hurt you."

The Lord had given me instructions concerning her through dreams, visions, and even an audible voice while I was waking out of my sleep.

I knew she would have the potential to help me build up myself; I also knew that there was a call on my life to serve the Lord. I can honestly say that it is better to serve the Lord as a single, consecrated man, than to choose a woman who makes your soul bitter and causes you to walk away from God.

I first saw this in her while we were in the courting stage, but it was on my honeymoon that it struck home to me. I was jokingly, though in my heart I was serious, trying to walk on water, and I told her to video it for me.

76

Though it was a fail, she turned to me and said, "Man of God, your faith will take you to great places." That may seem simple, but it was powerful for me.

After we got married, she would ask me questions about my plans and how I would go about achieving these things. If I came up with a plan, she would try to get the best out of it, no matter how simple it seemed.

The ministry that I started, "The 'Inna' Man," was established with the help of my wife and her obedience to the Lord. She also played a great role in the writing of this book. She places so much effort in the pictures I take, how I look, even with the posts I make on social media, she ensures that there are no errors in them. This woman covers me from all areas and angles.

Now my wife is a very powerful woman of God, and I know that the Lord has a very powerful ministry for her as well, but she honestly puts so much into my dreams and ministry.

Encouragement

The woman who a man chooses to marry is very important. I believe that many women have the potential to be builders, but they have to use their words as a tool over their household and not as a sword against others. You have to decide what you are going to use your word to do. If there were more of these women in our society, then it would be a much better place. Do you know how many women have destroyed their own children's destiny with their words because the fathers did them wrong? Women have even cursed their own children out of anger.

When the scripture says life and death are in the power of the tongue **(Proverbs 18:21 - KJV)**, it was revealing to you that God has given you power over your words. I encourage you to choose to use your tongue to build up and not destroy.

CHAPTER FOUR
"AS PRECIOUS AS GOLD"

THE TONGUE OF WISDOM

It takes a wise woman to preserve a nation and its people, but the foolish woman will destroy her own heritage and people.

There was an incident that took place in my life, and the only reason there was no major damage was because a wise woman was in the midst of my accusers.

Operations Of This Tongue

About four years ago, I was seeking the Lord, as usual, through prayer and fasting because I was asked to do a good deed for a friend. It so happened that this friend and I shared the responsibility over a house. Even before this happened, I cautioned my friend that these things normally destroyed friendships. However, we took a chance, and I decided that I could not turn my back on a friend in need.

We were sharing this place together when my friend decided that a family member, his sister, had some business to take care of. My friend's sister was supposed to be a newborn Christian, but she had a tongue of Asp, destruction and seduction. She would try to poison my

81

mind against my friend, and I never said anything to my friend for the sake of not ruining their relationship since the arrangement was temporary.

This continued to the point where my other friend was poisoned by her ways, and because I was not listening to her, she started sowing seeds of discord among us. So I went on a fast, repented, and sought the Lord. I was at the point where I told my friend that his sister had to leave because she was causing problems. However, it was ignored because I was still trying not to cause a problem between them.

One day I was seeking the Lord, and as I got out of prayer, I saw that my friend got a phone call and left for hours. As I sat in the chair, I suddenly felt my heart begin to sink, and I said, "Ah, my God, I feel heavy." I knew that trouble was coming against me.

Hours later, another friend arrived, then I saw two of my friends strolling in a few minutes later. Already I saw the play for me. The friend who had arrived first did this before to make it seem as if they were coming from different places.

Now one of my friends, the wise young lady, said to me, "Brother, I heard a thing, and I left my home to come all the way here, for I cannot believe what I am hearing." I allowed them to say what was being discussed. There were some railing accusations against me, but when I opened my mouth and began to speak, they realized that the accusations were all lies, and they were all gathered against me for nothing.

Two of my friends had decided not be my friend anymore, but the wise friend said, "Let us hear the matter before we come to that conclusion," for she was already aware of the ways of the other friend's sister. Her action helped restored our friendship, although it took a while for things to settle since their action against me was unjust. A wise person would not be quick to act on a one-sided argument.

This friend of mine used her tongue to demonstrate wisdom. My other friends told me that if this was not resolved, they would have ended our friendship on the basis that I was a deceiver and was acting like I was pure before God and so on. A woman with a wise tongue will seek to preserve and not destroy, and that is what this friend did.

"Every wise woman buildeth her house: but the foolish plucketh it down with her hands." (Proverbs 14:1 - KJV).

Wise Rebekah

In the book of Genesis, there is the story of Jacob and Esau. Now Esau was a strong man and a hunter. He looked so strong and manly to the point that his father loved him more. Now his twin brother, Jacob, was a skinny and flimsy-looking man, but his mother loved him more.

Rebekah had difficulties when she was pregnant with Jacob and Esau. The Lord revealed to her that she had two nations in her womb, and the elder would serve the younger.

"And the children struggled together within her; and she said, If it be so, why am I thus? And she went to enquire of the LORD. And the LORD said unto her, Two nations are in thy womb, and two manner of people shall be separated from thy bowels; and the one people shall be stronger than the other people; and the elder shall serve the younger." (Genesis 25:22-23 - KJV).

The prophecy was given to Rebekah that her children would be two nations, and the older would serve the younger. How was this even possible? Esau was the firstborn so he would have been in line for the blessings; however, God had another plan.

Esau was loved by his father a lot, but he was doing things that his parents, especially his mother, were not pleased with, like taking to himself women from the neighboring nations. This was a very serious thing to them as before Abraham died, he sent his servant to get a wife for his son, Isaac, all the way back to where he came from, and that wife was Rebekah.

Now Esau had also sold his birthright to Jacob one day for a bowl of stew, which means that he gave his brother the birthright blessings.

When I was younger, and my father told me this story, at first, he painted a picture that the woman caused the wrong person to get the blessings, but it was not so. The woman actually preserved the promise of God through her actions. She preserved the heritage of Israel as it was Jacob whose name was changed to Israel after an encounter with the Lord.

"And Rebekah spake unto Jacob her son, saying, Behold, I heard thy father speak unto Esau thy brother, saying, Bring me venison, and make me savoury meat, that I may eat, and bless thee before the LORD before my death. Now therefore, my son, obey my voice according to that which I command thee. Go now to the flock, and fetch me from thence two good kids of the goats; and I will make them savoury meat for thy father, such as he loveth: And thou shalt bring it to thy father, that he may eat, and that he may bless thee before his death. And Jacob said to Rebekah his mother, Behold, Esau my brother is a hairy man, and I am a smooth man: My father peradventure will feel me, and I shall seem to him as a deceiver; and I shall bring

a curse upon me, and not a blessing. And his mother said unto him, Upon me be thy curse, my son: only obey my voice, and go fetch me them." (Genesis 27:6-13 - KJV).

Jacob was so afraid to hearken unto his mother's request for him to deceive his father and to get the birthright blessings that was already given over to him by his brother, but his mother told him that if his father cursed him, then the curse should be upon her.

Rebekah was the one who carried both these children, and the Lord had already showed her what would become of them both. Esau was also a great nation and a people, but it was Jacob who the Lord would use to continue His promise. In fact, God called Himself the God of Abraham, Isaac, and Jacob, not Esau.

"And Esau hated Jacob because of the blessing wherewith his father blessed him: and Esau said in his heart, The days of mourning for my father are at hand; then will I slay my brother Jacob. And these words of Esau her elder son were told to Rebekah: and she sent and called Jacob her younger son, and said unto him, Behold, thy brother Esau, as touching thee, doth comfort himself, purposing to kill thee. Now therefore, my son, obey my voice; arise, flee thou to Laban my brother to Haran; And tarry with him a few days, until thy brother's fury turn away; Until thy brother's anger

turn away from thee, and he forget that which thou hast done to him: then I will send, and fetch thee from thence: why should I be deprived also of you both in one day? And Rebekah said to Isaac, I am weary of my life because of the daughters of Heth: if Jacob take a wife of the daughters of Heth, such as these which are of the daughters of the land, what good shall my life do me?" (Genesis 27:41-46 - KJV).

Rebekah further preserved Israel by sending away Jacob to take a wife from her birthplace, the same place that Isaac took her from. This was indeed the actions of a wise woman and not a deceiver. The fear of the Lord is the beginning of wisdom, and to know the Lord is understanding. Rebekah feared the Lord and, just like Mary, she kept the prophecy in her heart, and because of her actions, the Word of the Lord was fulfilled; now Israel is a great nation. They may have strayed from the true and living God, but they are still His people.

A wise woman will always make a decision to protect and preserve, even if it will cost her in the long run. Rebekah used her tongue in the way of wisdom. Wisdom is directional, and where there is wisdom, the people will not perish.

Acts of Wisdom

Another demonstration of the tongue of wisdom is with Hannah, the wife of Elkanah, who prayed to the Lord to open her womb that she may conceive a son. Now Elkanah loved Hannah the most of his two wives, but she was barren, and this bothered her. What she did was just amazing. She went and cried before the Lord and told the Lord that if He gave her a son, she would give him back to the Lord.

"So Hannah rose up after they had eaten in Shiloh, and after they had drunk. Now Eli the priest sat upon a seat by a post of the temple of the LORD. And she was in bitterness of soul, and prayed unto the LORD, and wept sore. And she vowed a vow, and said, O LORD of hosts, if thou wilt indeed look on the affliction of thine handmaid, and remember me, and not forget thine handmaid, but wilt give unto thine handmaid a man child, then I will give him unto the LORD all the days of his life, and there shall no razor come upon his head." (1 Samuel 1:9-11 - KJV).

One may ask, how is this a wise woman, and what did she preserve? Eli, who was the priest at that time, was old, and his sons who should have replaced him were very corrupted; they were not walking in the ways of God. Hannah kept Samuel as a Nazarite and gave him to the Lord. Samuel became one of the most powerful prophets in Israel, and the priesthood was consecrated again through him. It was Samuel who anointed the first king of Israel and set things in order as a judge in his time.

Hannah was indeed a wise woman. Her action caused something very amazing. She wanted a child and dedicated that one child to the Lord when he came of age, and the Lord blessed her with more children.

The actions of this wise woman brought forth a man who the Lord used to preserve a nation. She was wise in her words when she prayed to the Lord and promised to give her son to Him.

"God is within her, she will not fall; God will help her at break of day." (Psalm 46:5 - NIV).

In 1 Samuel 25, there was also a woman by the name of Abigail who saved the life of her foolish husband, Nabal. The anointed King David was trying to flee from Saul, who wanted to kill him, so he found himself in the wilderness. David and his men were watching over Nabal's sheep in the wilderness, and so he sent his men to Nabal for food because they were in the wilderness for so long and were very hungry. This was Nabal's reply:

"And Nabal answered David's servants, and said, Who is David? And who is the son of Jesse? There be many servants now a days that break away every man from his master. Shall I then take my bread, and my water, and my flesh that I have killed for my shearers, and give it unto men, whom I know not whence they be?" (1 Samuel 25:10-11 - KJV).

When David heard this response, he and his men were so angry that they were going to kill Nabal and destroy his entire household, but his wife, Abigail, saved him.

"And when Abigail saw David, she hasted, and lighted off the ass, and fell before David on her face, and bowed herself to the ground, And fell at his feet, and said, Upon me, my lord, upon me let this iniquity be: and let thine handmaid, I pray thee, speak in thine audience, and hear the words of thine handmaid. Let not my lord, I pray thee, regard this man of Belial, even Nabal: for as his name is, so is he; Nabal is his name, and folly is with him: but I thine handmaid saw not the young men of my lord, whom thou didst send. Now therefore, my lord, as the LORD liveth, and as thy soul liveth, seeing the LORD hath withholden thee from coming to shed blood, and from avenging thyself with thine own hand, now let thine enemies, and they that seek evil to my lord, be as Nabal. And now this blessing which thine handmaid hath brought unto my lord, let it even be given unto the young men that follow my lord." (1 Samuel 25:23-27 - KJV).

Abigail took some food and went in haste to present it before David. She spoke to him words of wisdom, and because of this, Nabal's life was spared. Nonetheless, Nabal eventually died because of his folly, and David took Abigail for his wife. David, being a wise man and one who sought God continually, knew the importance of having a wise woman in his life. This is how important it is to have a woman who speaks with wisdom. Her words to David preserved Nabal's life and prevented David from doing evil by killing him.

Such is the tongue of a wise woman. With all that she does, she preserves lives. She will not cause death but rather spare lives.

"She openeth her mouth with wisdom; and in her tongue is the law of kindness. She looketh well to the ways of her household, and eateth not the bread of idleness." (Proverbs 31:26-27 - KJV).

Another wise woman was Bathsheba, the mother of Solomon. God had promised David that Solomon, his son, would sit on the throne after he died. However, David's other son, Adonijah, went ahead and tried to take the throne in David's old age, without his knowledge.

At that time, it was Bathsheba who Nathan, the prophet, had to send to the king about the matter in order to preserve Israel. Solomon was who the Lord had chosen and not Adonijah; furthermore, if you took the kingdom without it being handed to you, that would be treason.

"And Bathsheba bowed, and did obeisance unto the king. And the king said, What wouldest thou? And she

said unto him, **My lord, thou swarest by the LORD thy God unto thine handmaid, saying, Assuredly Solomon thy son shall reign after me, and he shall sit upon my throne. And now, behold, Adonijah reigneth; and now, my lord the king, thou knowest it not: And he hath slain oxen and fat cattle and sheep in abundance, and hath called all the sons of the king, and Abiathar the priest, and Joab the captain of the host: but Solomon thy servant hath he not called." (1 Kings 1:16-19 - KJV).**

Bathsheba, through the directions of Nathan the prophet, went in to David and presented the matter before him. It was after this that the kingdom was saved from Adonijah, and Solomon ended up being the wisest and richest king in Israel; the king who built a house unto the Lord. A wise woman preserves what was built and does not allow it to be destroyed.

This is very serious as it takes wisdom for a woman to make some decisions. A man who has a wise woman for his wife is a man who will be secured. Wisdom is a chief thing that is to be desired more than silver and gold. Many people are able to build things, but not many are able to preserve it for generations to come.

Encouragement

Can you imagine if these women never acted in wisdom? An entire nation could not be preserved, and the promises of the Lord would have been further delayed.

As a woman, this is the type of person you should desire to be. You should desire to be the woman who preserves her heritage and save lives; and the woman who will not go to the ways of contention and destruction. A wise woman will know how to act and what to say at all times. She will not be given over to ignorance and folly.

At the beginning of this chapter, I shared the story of my friend who, through wisdom, preserved all our friendships. This young lady could have just believed what was said to her, but instead, she desired to know the truth.

Wisdom is a principal thing, and I would advise those who are reading this book to desire it. It is very important that a woman desires to have the tongue of wisdom; and as a man, this is the type of woman you should desire to marry so you can get Godly counsel.

CHAPTER FIVE
"AS PURE AS SILVER"

THE TONGUE OF SUBMISSION

Operations Of This Tongue

People often misinterpret a submissive woman as weak, but it takes great strength to be a submissive woman in today's society.

The order of authority is God, Christ, husband, then wife. Society has deceived women into believing that being submissive means that you are a full homemaker. This just means you would stay at home all day to take care of the children and cook and clean, so there is nothing else to life for you. That, my friend, is the biggest lie you have believed.

A submissive woman carries her husband and family in an even greater way than the builder and the wise woman. This woman is indeed endowed with wisdom; a woman who truly fears God has no trouble being submissive to her husband. She does not bring shame to her husband or family and is often the meekest among women.

Do you know that to be meek is to be submissive? Look at the horse and the jockey, for example. The horse's

97

mouth is bridled, so by pulling the bridle, the jockey directs the horse to victory. The horse that wins the race is considered to be the meekest horse.

A submissive woman truly has the quality of a queen. She endows her husband with respect, and because of her, many will also respect her husband.

"She maketh herself coverings of tapestry; her clothing is silk and purple. Her husband is known in the gates, when he sitteth among the elders of the land." (Proverbs 31:22-23 - KJV).

Even the elders of the land respect her husband. For some reason, I can guarantee you that it is not easy to find submissive women in western society. Western society has taught women that they do not need men and they do not need to respect their husbands for they are both equal and things are fifty-fifty. The truth is, things are not fifty-fifty when it comes to money and other things.

Men are also to be blamed for they have the most twisted idea of a submissive woman. Gentlemen, you will not get a woman to respect and submit herself to you through abusing her. For some reason, men in both the eastern and western societies think that submission means abuse and a woman should not speak. That is nonsense. If women were not made to speak, then they would not have a mouth.

Submission is the highest form of honor a woman can give to a man. The scripture teaches us as men to love our wives, and the wives should respect their husbands. Women already know how to love a man, but many do not understand that a woman's love for a man is demonstrated through respect. A man's love for a woman is demonstrated through caring, kindness, giving her attention, and making her feel important. For decades, our society has been openly and forcefully getting rid of this ordinance that was given, not from men, but from the Lord.

This is something I have been trying to understand for years: what is the submission of a wife to her husband? If I should say my mother was a submissive wife to my father because she cooked for him, took care of me and my siblings, and worked hard daily while doing this, then I would be adapting to society's mindset. At one point, my mother and father made us pray as a family before bed, and on Sundays, my mother would get us all dressed for church. All this was too much for her alone in the marriage, but society taught her that this is the role of a submissive woman while forgetting to tell my father to love and help her out too.

The idea of a woman doing so many things is not about submission but rather duties passed down through traditions. Some traditions are good, so I will not go against those. We have lost these traditions as a number of today's women are not familiar with the kitchen.

A woman who is able to manage her house and take care of her household should be commended, but that does not mean she respects her husband or is submissive to him. My mother was doing all of that, but she was grumbling in her heart and behind my father's back. This was a lot for any woman, and he should have helped her, but submission starts within the heart.

The children of Israel, when they were in the wilderness and even after, were considered rebellious and stiff-necked, for they were not submitted (yielded) to God from their hearts.

These women are very few these days because instead of following the ordinance of the scripture, people are now listening to the prophets on social media and big media giants who are suddenly experts on life. They believe they know more than the bible.

"Her children arise up, and call her blessed; her husband also, and he praiseth her. Many daughters have done virtuously, but thou excellest them all." (Proverbs 31:28-29 - KJV).

A very interesting thing I have noticed is that every woman wants to be a Proverbs 31 woman. Honestly, I would love if it was so, but this woman knows how to tame her tongue and conduct herself. The woman with the tongue of submission is the true Proverbs 31 woman. She is very wise and knows how to build.

The opposite of a submissive woman is a nagging and controlling woman. The scripture says it is better to live in the corner of a housetop than in a broad house with a contentious woman **(See Proverbs 24:4).** As a man, if you really want true peace and to avoid shame, then this is not the woman you want for your wife.

A number of women are soft-spoken, and people believe that this means they are submissive. This is a misconception. A submissive woman does speak with grace and gentleness, but she also knows how to speak with boldness.

"Favour is deceitful, and beauty is vain: but a woman that feareth the LORD, she shall be praised. Give her of the fruit of her hands; and let her own works praise her in the gates." (Proverbs 31:30-31 - KJV).

This is the woman who deserves to be greeted with praise, for she fears the Lord.

A number of women who were living with unsaved husbands before they became Christians are struggling in the area of submission and are not able to lead these men to Christ. As a woman, it will not be easy for you to lead a man to Christ by just preaching the Gospel to him, but he will recognize changes from the way you live your life. If that man is not able to see the light of God in you, you will not be able to lead him to Christ.

I have noticed that women can say the meanest things, and no matter what a man says to hurt a woman, whatever she says will hurt him more. Some women, instead of using their tongues to submit themselves to their husbands, use their tongue to tell the husband how terrible he is. A woman who is really submitted to God would ask God to set watch over her mouth and keep the doors of her life.

A friend of mine once shared a story with me, and I honestly do not know how I would expect a woman to act in this situation, but this woman acted in a way that was just mind-blowing.

This woman became a Christian, and because of this, her husband decided that he was going to test her patience. However, she tried her best not to answer her husband the way she normally would. Whatever she did, he would make it a problem, and she would just hold her peace and get it done his way. It got to the point where she gave him a cup of tea, and he got angry and threw it on her, and it burned one of her arms, and she just made him another cup and went out the door to church. The man then turned up to the church in tears, declaring that his wife is a true Christian, and confessed all he was doing to break her. He ended up receiving life from the Lord, for truly we are the ones receiving life and not we giving our lives to Christ; if you are not in Christ, you are dead.

Look at this woman, for instance, I know more than enough women of God who would have started tussling with this man. I am not saying a woman should make a man abuse her, but I am showing you how a submissive woman won her husband over to the kingdom of the Lord by her actions and how she spoke to him. The scripture says that he who wins souls is wise **(See Proverbs 11:30)**. This woman demonstrated great wisdom. A woman with a submissive tongue has learned self-control.

My pastor, who counseled my wife and me before we got married, taught us that we were serving each other once married. We would now have to think more about the other person than our own self and try to serve that person.

A woman with a submissive tongue listens more than how she speaks and is not given over to her emotions.

People treat submission as if it is a gift, but the problem is, the older women have failed to teach the younger women how to behave and conduct themselves.

"The aged women likewise, that they be in behaviour as becometh holiness, not false accusers, not given to much wine, teachers of good things; That they may teach the young women to be sober, to love their husbands, to love their children, To be discreet, chaste, keepers at home, good, obedient to their own husbands, that the word of God be not blasphemed." (Titus 2:3-5 - KJV).

The scripture says women are to be obedient to their own husbands. Do you know that a number of women are more obedient to their pastors than their husbands? Their husbands would give them wise counsel, and they reject it and accept the same counsel from their pastors.

According to the scripture, the older women must teach the younger women. A submissive woman will always live as unto God in holiness. Sometimes I hear my mother-in-law asking my wife on the phone if she is taking care of me, and it makes me feel so special. I interpret that as even my mother-in-law respects me.

When I was migrating to be with my wife in her country of birth, her mother helped her to prepare such a welcome for me to the point where I felt so special and loved. Her mother was passing down these teachings to her.

In the book of Genesis, Sarah, the wife of Abraham, is one I would consider a submissive woman.

"But let it be the hidden man of the heart, in that which is not corruptible, even the ornament of a meek and quiet spirit, which is in the sight of God of great price. For after this manner in the old time the holy women also, who trusted in God, adorned themselves, being in subjection unto their own husbands: Even as Sara obeyed Abraham, calling him lord: whose daughters ye are, as long as ye do well, and are not afraid with any amazement. (1 Peter 3:4-6 - KJV).

The scripture here is showing us how Sarah demonstrated respect for her husband even in the way she addressed him. In the book of Genesis, when the Lord came to visit Abraham, Sarah went to prepare something for the Lord to eat. Some women, when their husbands have guests over, do not even try to make the guests speak well of their husbands by offering them something to eat or drink.

Submissive Sarah

"And there was a famine in the land: and Abram went down into Egypt to sojourn there; for the famine was grievous in the land. And it came to pass, when he was

105

come near to enter into Egypt, that he said unto Sarai his wife, Behold now, I know that thou art a fair woman to look upon: Therefore it shall come to pass, when the Egyptians shall see thee, that they shall say, This is his wife: and they will kill me, but they will save thee alive. Say, I pray thee, thou art my sister: that it may be well with me for thy sake; and my soul shall live because of thee. And it came to pass, that, when Abram was come into Egypt, the Egyptians beheld the woman that she was very fair. (Genesis 12:10-14 - KJV).

The submissive woman is truly like a queen. Sarah was such a submissive woman. Her husband, knowing that she was such a beautiful woman, thought that the Egyptians would want to kill him for his wife. So Abraham reasoned with his wife and told her to tell them that she was his sister, so they would not kill him. Now because of her submission to her husband, she actually saved his life. Some may ask, was Abraham not telling her to lie? The case is not so in this matter, so she was indeed his sister as much as she was his wife.

My wife and I were reasoning about a matter earlier this year, and she brought to me the scripture in Titus 2 about the older women teaching the younger to be obedient to their husbands. As she read it, she admitted that when women first hear the word to be obedient to their husbands, many will interpret it wrong. However, if you cannot submit to your husband, you are not pleasing God.

You cannot please God fully if as a woman you have a powerful ministry, but you are not submissive to your husband. My wife could not learn fully what a submissive wife is until she met her husband. For this reason, the older women are to teach the younger so they are being prepared for marriage.

Another instance of Sarah's submission was in a similar scenario with King Abimelech.

"And Abraham journeyed from thence toward the south country, and dwelled between Kadesh and Shur, and sojourned in Gerar. And Abraham said of Sarah his wife, She is my sister: and Abimelech king of Gerar sent, and took Sarah." (Genesis 20:1-2 - KJV).

When Sarah told Pharaoh in Genesis 12 that Abraham was her brother, Pharaoh actually gave Abraham riches and goods because he wanted Abraham's wife. The Lord had come against Egypt that they would not touch Sarah or Abraham, and they sent them away with their riches and goods.

In chapter 20, the Lord visited Abimelech in a dream so he would not touch Sarah. However, because of Sarah's submissiveness to her husband, she spared his life and caused him to get much wealth.

"Then Abimelech called Abraham, and said unto him, What hast thou done unto us? And what have I offended thee, that thou hast brought on me and on my kingdom a great sin? Thou hast done deeds unto me that ought not to be done. And Abimelech said unto Abraham, What sawest thou, that thou hast done this thing? And Abraham said, Because I thought, Surely the fear of God is not in this place; and they will slay me for my wife's sake. And yet indeed she is my sister; she is the daughter of my father, but not the daughter of my mother; and she became my wife. And it came to pass, when God caused me to wander from my father's house, that I said unto her, This is thy kindness which thou shalt shew unto me; at every place whither we shall come, say of me, He is my brother. And Abimelech took sheep, and oxen, and menservants, and womenservants, and gave them unto Abraham, and restored him Sarah his wife. And Abimelech said, Behold, my land is before thee: dwell where it pleaseth thee. And unto Sarah he said, Behold, I have given thy brother a thousand pieces of silver: behold, he is to thee a covering of the eyes, unto all that are with thee, and with all other: thus she was reproved." (Genesis 20:9-16 - KJV).

A submissive woman, by far, is not a weak woman. It was this same Sarah who, when she had told Abraham to lie with her maid, Hagar, for she was not able to give her a son, later told him to send away the woman and her child. Now when Abraham complained about this, the Lord told him to hearken unto his wife. This was not a weak woman. She knew how to love and honor her husband and when she corrected him, the Lord stood with her.

Submissiveness adds to the beauty of a woman. When a woman is submissive, she will attract the favor of the Lord.

A disobedient wife will destroy not only her husband but also herself.

In the same book of Genesis, when the Lord was about to destroy Sodom and Gomorrah, the Angel of the Lord told Lot to get his family out of the city, and not one of them should look back. Lot's wife, in her disobedience, looked back. Now, if this woman had obeyed her husband's instruction which was given to him by the angel, she would not have turned into a pillar of salt.

A disobedient woman is a danger to herself, and she does not even know it.

Submission takes into account how you speak, respond and even behave towards the person who is set over you. It was for this reason that Paul encouraged wives to submit to their own husbands. Submission is first a state of the heart. It is a struggle for many women and men.

When Ruth laid at Boaz's feet, that was an act of yielding herself to him **(See Ruth 3:14).** The acts she did were her way of saying, "I submit to you."

This will not be easy for many women, and even men, but as a wife, you must learn submission and make it find a place in your heart. Wives are called to respect their husbands; submission to your husband is the highest form of respect to him.

Encouragement

"And Samuel said, Hath the LORD as great delight in burnt offerings and sacrifices, as in obeying the voice of the LORD? Behold, to obey is better than sacrifice, and to hearken than the fat of rams." (1 Samuel 15:22 - KJV).

As a woman, you can do a million different things to please your husband. You can make as many sacrifices as you want to, but nothing shows your husband that you love him more than when you are submissive. You know, a lot of women do so much, and many do not understand that a woman who truly pleases the Lord is the crown of her husband.

The man who cannot understand the ways of a submissive woman is a very foolish and misguided man. He who abuses any woman is in danger of God, but the man who dares to lift his hand at this kind of woman will surely be cut down to nothing faster than he can take the next breath.

Ladies, this is the type of woman you should aspire to be. Society will never understand your ways, neither will they be able to comprehend who you are, but many will aspire in their hearts to be like you. You will be the woman who has control over her heart, mind, and spirit. A submissive woman is not a weak woman; she is the perfect wife.

CHAPTER SIX
"DEEPER THINGS"

AUTHOR'S FINAL THOUGHTS

Now that you have read the first five chapters, I hope I got you to the place where if you are a woman, you realize that you do not want to be a poisonous, destructive woman, and as a man, you do not want to be the fool anymore. I pray that your hearts have been moved to the point where you desire to be the woman who builds and preserves lives and an inheritance.

Take Job's wife, for example, in the book of Job. Her husband was suffering, and instead of trying to encourage him, she attacked him and was telling him to forget about his integrity and just curse God and die. What type of woman tells a man to curse God and die? You do not want to be this foolish woman, nor should any man consider her for a wife.

What will it be?

"See, I have this day set thee over the nations and over the kingdoms, to root out, and to pull down, and to

**destroy, and to throw down, to build, and to plant."
(Jeremiah 1:10 - KJV).**

With your tongue, you can do any of the above as stated
in Jeremiah 1:10. However, when you choose to give life
and build, then you will be much more valuable to life
and the continuation of people. As a woman who has
read the five chapters, you should choose to be a
combination of the last three. You want to be a wise,
submissive woman who builds up her household and
descendants.

Women are very influential and have been since creation.
One way or another, women were involved where there
was greatness. I believe the Lord led me to write this
book to open your eyes and to empower you because
future generations are depending on you to use your
influence for good.

Something Deeper

As I am growing in the Lord, I have come to realize that
the Lord is raising up some powerful women in today's
society. I wondered and asked the Lord about this, and
He opened my eyes to something even greater.

As a woman, you have no idea how important you are to
God and the great task He would have you to do in this
time. The Lord is pouring out His Spirit on a number of
women all around the world to be empowered to engage

116

in this fight. A type of Deborah anointing is being poured out on our women, so they can use their voices and influence to do good.

Women have played a great role in this present world, but because of the Jezebel spirit upon the feminist movement, many women have been blinded to what is happening. I implore you to learn of biblical femininity, and you can be a woman without feeling like you need to compete with a man.

The rise of the Jezebel spirit has been trying to remove men as the head of the household, and we see how that is damaging our society. However, now more than ever, women are being removed from their positions without even noticing. They are advocating for trans-athletes; women have fought hard for them to be able to compete in male-dominated sports. Now men who are identified as women are taking that over, not to mention a trans-boxer who is beating up women in the ring. Psychology will tell you that this is one way an abusive man can abuse women without having to be stigmatized as abusive. They are now at the point where they want men who claim to be women to use the same restroom as your daughters.

If our women do not rise up in this hour, then they will lose everything they have fought for. I pray for your eyes to be opened.

Did you know that life begins before the womb? For all you pro-choice women, I want you to take a minute and pay attention to this mystery.

There was a story of a woman who had an abortion before her second child was born, and the child came to her mother with some questions that would even trouble the most sophisticated minds. One day this child came to her mother and asked her about her sister, telling her what she was going to name her and other plans she had for this child before the abortion. The mother asked her how she knew all this, and she said she met her. Now this child was not born, but she is well alive.

"Before I formed thee in the belly I knew thee...." (Jeremiah 1:5a - KJV).

Before God formed you in your mother's womb, He knew you. If you believe that God is real, then you must believe that if God knew you before you were born, then you existed before you were born.

Life does not begin in the natural; it begins in the spiritual realm. So when a child is aborted, that child's earthly temple is destroyed, and he or she is blocked from entering the earth realm.

The womb of the woman is a doorway between the natural and the spiritual realm. This is the reason why a

118

lot of women come under so much attack. From the prophecy was released in Genesis 3, the enemy has launched a war against the woman in so many ways.

"And I will put enmity between thee and the woman, and between thy seed and her seed; it shall bruise thy head, and thou shalt bruise his heel." (Genesis 3:15 - KJV).

Satan is afraid of the seed that you will bring into this world. When a woman does an abortion, she is coming in agreement with Satan's plan to destroy mankind.

The child that you carry will be used by God to do great things on this earth, and that is what the devil is afraid of.

A baby's heartbeat is detected at six weeks, not because a heart was not there before the six weeks, but because it is so small to detect. The heart is one of the first things that develops because that is where the soul is placed.

"And Mary arose in those days, and went into the hill country with haste, into a city of Juda; And entered into the house of Zacharias, and saluted Elisabeth. And it came to pass, that, when Elisabeth heard the salutation of Mary, the babe leaped in her womb; and Elisabeth was filled with the Holy Ghost: And she spake out with a loud voice, and said, Blessed art thou among women,

and blessed is the fruit of thy womb. And whence is this to me, that the mother of my Lord should come to me? For, lo, as soon as the voice of thy salutation sounded in mine ears, the babe leaped in my womb for joy. (Luke 1:39-44 - KJV).

The Lord Jesus Christ, when He was in Mary's womb and when Mary went to visit Elizabeth, was not even a full month in His mother's womb, yet at Mary's greeting, John was filled with the Holy Ghost. Elizabeth uttered praises for she knew the Lord was in Mary's womb. Can you imagine that persons want to abort a child who has matured up to the stage of birth? This is murder, and we are kindling the anger of God against mankind.

"My substance was not hid from thee, when I was made in secret, and curiously wrought in the lowest parts of the earth. Thine eyes did see my substance, yet being unperfect; and in thy book all my members were written, which in continuance were fashioned, when as yet there was none of them." (Psalm 139:15 - KJV).

God knew every one of your days, even before you lived them. Many are spiritually blind and are not discerning these things. If our women do not rise up in this season and use their tongue to preserve our children's future, then a lot of people are going to be living with regrets.

CHAPTER SEVEN
"PERFECT FREEDOM"

RENUNCIATION AND DECLARATIONS

Prayer Of Salvation

I f you are not a Christian and you have never confessed the Lord Jesus Christ, now is the time. If you have not been living as a woman of God, now is the time to give yourself back to the Lord.

Father, in the name of the Lord Jesus Christ, I come before You confessing that I am a sinner in need of Your salvation. Father, please forgive me of all my sins and my unrighteousness, please, good Father, deliver me from these bondages and chains of sin and set me free. Father, I have lived wickedly and think myself to be a good person, but now I know that only You are good. I believe Jesus Christ is the Son of God, who died on the Cross of Calvary and rose again the third day and lives forever. I come to You today, Lord, that You would wash me in the Blood of Jesus Christ and translate me from this darkness into Your marvelous kingdom. Good Father, here I am, take my life today. I surrender completely; please come and abide inside of my heart and teach me Your good ways. As of today, Lord, my life is now Yours, and Your vows are upon me until death. In the Lord Jesus Christ's mighty name, I pray with all my heart and believe You are my Lord and God. Amen.

"Jesus answered, Verily, verily, I say unto thee, Except a man be born of water and of the Spirit, he cannot enter into the kingdom of God." (John 3:5 - KJV).

Now that you have said the prayer, you must be baptized of the water. Find a church that preaches the Bible completely or a believer filled with the Holy Spirit to baptize you in water.

"Then Peter said unto them, Repent, and be baptized every one of you in the name of Jesus Christ for the remission of sins, and ye shall receive the gift of the Holy Ghost." (Acts 2:38 - KJV).

The Lord promised the gift of the Holy Spirit, and without the Holy Spirit, you are going to have a more challenging life than it ought to be. The baptism of the Holy Spirit is essential to living this Christian life.

I pray this over you:

I declare the fire of God that breaks chains will fall upon you now, in the mighty name of the Lord Jesus Christ! I declare you are washed by the Blood of Jesus, and there is therefore no condemnation to you! I pray God will now baptize you with the fire of the Holy Ghost to make you equipped for this the end times! In the mighty name of the Lord Jesus Christ, let it be so! Amen.

124

Renunciation

If you have done or contributed to any abortion, just say this prayer before we go into the renunciations:

Father, please forgive me for destroying the precious life of Your children that You have given me. I was foolish and without understanding, but I ask You to forgive me, heal and deliver me from the guilt of blood. In the Lord Jesus' Name, set me free. Amen.

- In the name of the Lord Jesus Christ, I renounce being a tool of the devil.
- In the name of the Lord Jesus Christ, I renounce and break the hold of the spirit of Jezebel over my life.
- In the name of the Lord Jesus Christ, I renounce and denounce the spirit of jealousy, envy, and contention.
- In the name of the Lord Jesus Christ, I renounce the spirit of seduction.
- In the name of the Lord Jesus Christ, I renounce destruction.
- In the name of the Lord Jesus Christ, I renounce every wicked ways.
- In the name of the Lord Jesus Christ, I renounce the antichrist.
- In the name of the Lord Jesus Christ, I renounce and denounce every curse that I have caused to leave my mouth to speak.

- In the name of the Lord Jesus Christ, I renounce and denounce my involvement in every occult practice.
- In the name of the Lord Jesus Christ, I renounce the spirit of control and rebellion.
- In the name of the Lord Jesus Christ, I renounce the spirit of disobedience.
- I plead the blood of Jesus Christ against every door in my life that is giving the enemy access to my life and command them to be closed as of today.
- I plead the blood of Jesus Christ over my life to seal me in His salvation and kingdom.

Declaration:

- In the name of the Lord Jesus Christ, I declare that I am now a child of God.
- In the name of the Lord Jesus Christ, I declare that my tongue is surrendered to the Lord Jesus Christ.
- In the name of the Lord Jesus Christ, I declare that my body is the temple of the Holy Ghost.
- In the name of the Lord Jesus Christ, I declare that I will use my tongue to build up.
- In the name of the Lord Jesus Christ, I declare that I will use my tongue to speak wisdom.
- In the name of the Lord Jesus Christ, I declare that I will use my tongue in the path of obedience.

- In the name of the Lord Jesus Christ, I declare that I will speak life and not death.
- In the name of the Lord Jesus Christ, I declare that I will be a woman who fears the Lord and protects my inheritance.

May the Lord bless and keep you in His perfect peace. May your life be a blessing, and because you have read this book, may wisdom and understanding be your portion. In the name of the Lord Jesus Christ, be blessed.

ABOUT THE AUTHOR

AB Harris, born Andrew Harris, is the founder of "The 'Inna' Man Ministries," a strength-based ministry that seeks to help Christians and unbelievers know the ways of the Lord Jesus Christ perfectly. He is a servant, husband, and father. Andrew has worked as a journalist in print media for over seven years and is a graduate of the University of Technology, Jamaica.

AB Harris has been serving the Lord seriously for more than six years after a radical life-changing encounter. He is called to prepare God's people in these last days and to raise up a holy generation unto God. He is also called to make intercession for the nations and impart wisdom to the people.

NOTES

NOTES

NOTES

www.ingramcontent.com/pod-product-compliance
Lightning Source LLC
LaVergne TN
LVHW051247080426
835513LV00016B/1780